The Xenophobe's® Guide to The Germans

Stefan Zeidenitz
Ben Barkow

D1040686

O

Oval Books

Published by Oval Books
335 Kennington Road
London SE11 4QE
United Kingdom

Telephone: +44 (0)20 7582 7123
Fax: +44 (0)20 7582 1022
E-mail: info@ovalbooks.com
Web site: www.ovalbooks.com

First published by Ravette Publishing, 1993
Reprinted/updated: 1994,1995,1996,1997,1998

First published by Oval Books, 1999
Updated 2000, reprinted 2001
Revised 2002, reprinted 2003
Updated 2005

Series Editor – Anne Tauté

Cover designer – Jim Wire, Quantum
Printer – Cox & Wyman Ltd
Producer – Oval Projects Ltd

Xenophobe's® is a Registered Trademark.

ISBN-13: 978-1-902825-29-2
ISBN-10: 1-902825-29-2

Contents

Nationalism and Identity 5

Character 11

Beliefs and Values 16

Behaviour 21

Manners 24

Obsessions 28

Leisure and Pleasure 30

Sense of Humour 33

Culture 36

Conversation and Gestures 40

Custom and Tradition 42

Eating and Drinking 44

Health and Hygiene 47

Systems 52

Government 56

Crime and Punishment 58

Business 59

Language and Ideas 62

'Cementing two nations together doesn't come cheap, especially when one of them (in estate agent terminology) "needs attention"…'

The population of the reunified Germans is 82 million (compared with 5 million Danes, 7 million Swiss, 8 million Austrians, 10 million Czechs, 10 million Belgians, 15 million Dutch, 38 million Poles, 50 million English, 58 million French and 293 million Americans).

Germany is nearly three times as big as England, but could fit into France 1½ times.

Nationalism and Identity

Forewarned or Wurst Case Scenario

The prospect of the Germans may cause even the devoted xenophobe to break stride. Viewed by some as a nation of square-jawed robots whose language sounds like something awful in the drains, whose cars out-perform all others and whose football team seldom loses, the Germans seem unassailable.

But behind the façade lies a nation distinctly uncertain about where it is, where it is going, even how it got there. Seeking refuge from the world's uncertainties, on the one hand they rely on order and system, the State and the Bundesbank; on the other they retreat into the *Angst* of the soul, psychoanalysis and high culture.

None of this anxiety should be mocked; humour is a quite separate category to be viewed in a serious light.

For the Germans, life is made up of two halves: the public and the private. The public sphere of jobs, official-dom, business and bureaucracy is radically different from the private one of family, friends, hobbies and holidays. What is fitting in the one is quite impossible in the other. In public, po-faced propriety is the order of the day. In private, shell-suited eccentricity abounds.

As a foreigner you will, almost by definition, encounter public Germany first, and may never see more. This explains something of their reputation abroad. All those sausages, all that beer.

Now that German consolidation has become a reality, even non-xenophobes fear for the future. The Germans themselves are not so much fearful of foreigners as fearful of any foreign country getting a bad impression of them. German industrial and financial might causes the uneasy national conscience to stir. Are we becoming arrogant? Is our tolerance failing? Are we on the slippery slope that could lead back to the bad old days? There aren't any firm answers to these questions, but the Germans, Europe's neurotics, crave answers.

If experience has taught them one thing, it is that there is no future outside the community of nations. No other nation has a stronger sense of the importance of getting along with others. Tolerance is not only a virtue, it's a duty.

How Others See Them

The emotions which the Germans arouse in others oscillate between admiration and fear – they are said to be either 'at your knees or at your throat'. They are thought of as efficient, self-obsessed, arrogant and domineering – altogether too good at finance and manufacturing.

To the British the Germans can seem lacking in the decencies of reserve and stiff upper lip. But they have always had a high regard for German cleverness and thoroughness, somehow imagining that of all Europeans, the Germans are most like themselves. This quaint illusion probably has its roots in the fact that so many Germans have occupied the British throne or been powers behind it. The fact is that the Germans are nothing like the British, couldn't be more different.

Take the most obvious example: British national identity was laid down somewhere around the time of the Roman invasion, and despite the occasional blip, hasn't really felt the need to question itself since. Germany, on the other hand, became a nation in the 1870s when it was effectively conquered from within by Iron Chancellor Bismarck of Prussia. Most Germans still place more importance on regional loyalties, and these days will rank being German a poor third after being, say, Swabian first and European second.

The French regard the Germans with suspicion and a measure of loathing, and seek to contain them by chumming-up. The Italians are dumbfounded by the Germans' capacity to get things done without bribing anyone, but regard them as utterly lacking in style.

For the Austrians a good German is one who is far away – preferably across the Atlantic, or even further. While they recognize that there is a cultural affinity between Vienna and Berlin, there is no affinity at all with their immediate neighbours, the Bavarians.

The Swiss see the Germans as being basically on the right lines, but needing to try a little harder (after all, in Switzerland you may be fined for using the wrong colour plastic sack to put your rubbish in, in Germany you are only fined for not using one).

How They See Others

The Germans generally adore the British and have suffered in the past from unrequited love. Britain used to be the ultimate role model with its amazingly advanced political, social, industrial and technological achievements. The Germans regard the British as being very nice and mostly harmless. Almost German.

They admire Americans for their (un-German) easygoing pragmatism and dislike them for their (un-German) superficiality. For the Germans, the United States is the headmaster in the school of nations, and accorded due respect if not always affection. Germans are strong believers in authority. 'If you know how to obey then you too can be a master' runs the refrain.

With the Italians Germans have a close understanding because they have so much history in common. Through wars, invasion and other forms of tourism, a deep and lasting friendship has been established. Italian art treasures, food and beaches are thoroughly appreciated. There is also a connection arising from the fact that Italy and Germany both achieved nationhood in the 19th century, and are still not entirely sure that this was a good thing.

The French are admired for their sophisticated civilization, and pitied for their inferior culture. The French may have higher spirits, but the Germans have deeper souls. Despite this, Francophilia is widespread among Germans, especially those living close to the French border.

Like a wistful child looking over the garden fence, the Germans envy Mediterranean people for their more relaxed attitudes, cultural heritage and warm climate. But only when they are on holiday.

The only people to whom the Germans readily concede unquestioned superiority of Teutonic virtues are the Swiss. No German would argue their supremacy in the fields of order, punctuality, diligence, cleanliness and thoroughness. They have never been to war with the Swiss.

How They See Themselves

Generally speaking, the Germans regard themselves as modest, rather ordinary sort of people. Give them a beer, a *Wurst*, a bit of *Gemütlichkeit* (cosiness) and another German with whom to argue politics or bemoan the stress of life, and they will be content. They are not greedy, do not expect something for nothing, and pay their bills on time. Simple, honest *Volk*.

They like to see themselves as romantic – not in a Mediterranean flowery-compliments-and-bottom-pinching way, but in the stormy genius mode. In every German there is a touch of the wild-haired Beethoven striding through forests and weeping over a mountain sunset, grappling against impossible odds to express the inexpressible. This is the Great German Soul, prominent display of which is essential whenever Art, Feeling and Truth are under discussion. After all, if the Germans did not actually invent the Romantic Movement (though they are pretty sure they did), they at least kitted it out with a lot of appropriately fraught and complicated philosophy.

They value themselves as diligent, thorough, orderly, reliable, methodical. They also see themselves as profoundly well educated. Contrary to popular belief, the Germans do not know everything, they just know everything better.

Special Relationships

Before the 1990s all West Germans were passionately keen on the idea of the two Germanys coming together again. How, they asked themselves and each other, can we find fulfilment as a nation while the great German *Geist* (spirit) is divided by a concrete wall?

All were agreed that reunification was a historical necessity. The same sort of consensus never existed *drüben* (over there), where people generally coveted the consumer durables but had their doubts about life in a society without ideological commitments. Now that unification is a fact, West Germans have their doubts, too.

All Wessies (former West Germans) know that all Ossies (former East Germans) are idle and complaining. All Ossies know that all Wessies are cynical and deceitful. It was ever so.

Cementing two nations together doesn't come cheap, especially when one of them (in estate agent terminology) 'needs attention' and has many 'period details' and 'original features'. In order to cope, the Germans set up The Trust Authority (*Treuhand*), which instantly became the world's largest employer, with 9,000 companies, nearly two million hectares of farm land and two million hectares of forest under its control. Its job was to privatize as much as it could, and shut down the rest.

Needless to say, the work of the *Treuhand* created suspicion among eastern Germans, who felt that their economic assets were being sold at knock-down prices, while they were treated as second-class citizens. Tension between the two kinds of Germans remains tangible, with some people now wondering if reunification was such a historical necessity after all, and if the Wall hadn't been the backbone of the great German *Geist* – only the politicians had been too stupid to realize it.

More than a decade on, some of the shine has come off the reunification. To many in the West, Eastern Germany seems a bottomless pit swallowing their Euros. At the same time, some in the eastern part feel that stagnation is now the gross national product and that, far from being in a state of transition, theirs has become a second class country for good.

Ever since the Change, Germans have suffered *Angst* like never before, and the soul-searching has taken on epic proportions. The effect has been to deepen German commitment to the ideals of the European Community still further; it offers a stable context for the turmoil within. Secretly some wish they had never embarked on this adventure and yearn for the old days, when life seemed simple and you knew who your enemies were.

How They Would Like Others to See Them

The Germans long to be understood and liked by others, yet secretly take pride that this can never be. After all, how can outsiders understand such a complex, deep, sensitive people? What can they know of the German struggle for identity or the tortured German spirit searching for release?

They would like to be respected for their devotion to truth and honesty. They are surprised that this is sometimes taken as tactlessness, or worse. After all, if I know you to be in error, surely it is my duty to correct you? Surely the Truth is more important than pretending to like your ghastly shirt or sports coat? Foreigners just cannot seem to appreciate this.

Dismissing German introspection as navel-gazing is taken as proof of shallowness. Complaints about German rudeness show misunderstanding. The Germans console themselves with the thought that devotion to higher causes and being true to the demands of the inner self are bound to rub a few people up the wrong way. It is sad, but quite unalterable. A good German wears his *Weltschmerz* (world-pain) on his sleeve and doesn't really mind being misunderstood.

Character

The Importance of Being *Ernsthaft*

In Germany, life is serious, and so is everything else. Outside Berlin, even humour is no laughing matter, and if you want to tell a joke you may want to submit a written application first.

The Germans strongly disapprove of the irrelevant, the flippant, the accidental. Serendipity is not a word in their language. The reason for this is that such things are not *ernsthaft*, serious. It is hardly conceivable (and certainly not desirable) that a good idea might arise by chance or come from somebody lacking the proper qualifications. On the whole Germans would prefer to forgo a clever invention rather than admit that creativity is a random and chaotic process.

Because life is *ernsthaft*, the Germans go by the rules. Schiller wrote, 'obedience is the first duty', and no German has ever doubted it. This fits with their sense of order and duty. Germans hate breaking rules, which can make life difficult because, as a rule, everything not expressly permitted is prohibited. If you are allowed to smoke or walk on the grass, a sign will inform you of this.

In professional life, devotion to earnestness means that you cannot give up accountancy or computer engineering in mid-life and switch to butterfly farming or aromatherapy. Any such change of heart would cause you to be dismissed as lightweight and unreliable.

Order

The Germans pride themselves on their efficiency, organization, discipline, cleanliness and punctuality. These are all manifestations of *Ordnung* which doesn't just mean tidiness, but correctness, properness, appropriateness and a host of other good things. No phrase warms the heart of a German like '*alles in Ordnung*', meaning everything is all right, everything is as it should be. The categorical imperative which no German escapes is '*Ordnung muss sein*', Order Must Be.

Germans like things that work. This is fundamental. A car or a washing machine which breaks down six months after purchase is not a nuisance, it's a breach of the social contract. They are mystified when they go abroad and see grimy buildings, littered streets, unwashed cars. On the platforms of the London underground they while away the hours between trains puzzling about why the crazy English put up with it and don't organize things properly. Even their language is unreliable and full of tricks, with people called 'Fanshaw' who spell their names Featherstonehaugh, and towns called Slough – which unaccountably rhymes with 'plough' and not with 'through' (which would make it Sloo) or 'enough' (Sluff).

In Germany, they manage these things better. Words may be long and guttural, but there are no tricks to pronunciation – what you see is what you get. The streets are clean, the houses painted, the litter in the bins. *Ordnung*.

Getting it Sorted

If you offer a German a piece of advice like 'Leave well enough alone' or 'If it ain't broke, don't fix it', they will assume you are British, or in need of psychotherapeutic aid.

It is axiomatic in Germany that everything needs sorting before you can achieve anything: the good needs to be sifted from the bad, the necessary from the contingent. What is yours must be clearly separated from what is mine; the public must be demarcated to prevent it getting confused with the private, the true must at all costs be distinguished from the false. Reliable definitions must be drawn up regarding what is masculine and what feminine (not to mention the characteristic German complication of the neuter). It goes on and on.

Only when everything is comprehensively compartmentalised can anything truly be said to be *in Ordnung*. This is the famous categorical imperative – ordered by Kant because he couldn't stand the undifferentiated hotchpotch of the world. Kant was determined, as no German had been before, to divide everything into distinct categories. He was notorious for driving his friends round the bend with his obsessive splitting of everything into smaller and smaller groups or classifications. In his library each volume formed a unique class which had to be kept in isolation in case any of the others contaminated its taxonomic distinctness. He went so far as to conceive a monumental plan in which all his books would be cut up and rebound so that their constituent words could be sorted and brought together – volumes full of correctly arranged 'the's' and 'and's' and so forth. He only abandoned this masterpiece of *Ordnung* when doing so was made a condition of his release back into the community.

The modern German does not go to such extremes, but only because such extremes have been sorted into a phenomenological phylum of the lunatic fringe, a nomenclatural subdivision few wish to be associated with.

Angst

Predictably, in their immaculate garden lurks a serpent: doubt. As a nation the Germans are racked with doubt and fight constantly to keep chaos at bay. Being German, they cannot brush their doubts aside or put off worrying in favour of a pint and a laugh. Not for them the touching British faith that it 'will be all right on the night', that it 'all comes out in the wash'. For a German, doubt and anxiety expand and ramify the more you ponder them. They are astonished that things haven't gone to pot already, and are pretty certain that they soon will.

Germany is, after all, the Land of *Angst*.

This leads to a certain reluctance to undertake anything. One 19th-century visitor to Germany remarked: '...they find obstacles to all; you hear "it is impossible" a hundred times... when action is necessary, the Germans know not how to struggle with difficulties.'

The Germans are aware of this, but see their anxiety as proportional to their intellectual capabilities. *Angst* is responsible for their desire that everything be regulated, controlled, checked, checked again, supervised, insured, examined, documented. Secretly, they believe it takes a superior intelligence to realize just how dangerous life really is.

Life's a Beach

The German craving for security is nowhere more evident than during holidays at the seaside. Here they have earned for themselves global notoriety for their ruthless efficiency in appropriating the best spots on the world's beaches.

No matter how early you struggle to get to the beach, the Germans will be there before you. Quite how they manage it remains a mystery, given that they can be seen carousing in the bars and tavernas until the small hours along with everyone else.

Having gained their beachheads, the Germans will immediately start digging in, constructing fortifications. You can always tell the beaches under German occupation: huge sandcastles cover the area, one per family, each several feet high, elaborately decorated with seashells and decaying starfish, crowned by flags.

Unlike everyone else, the Germans prefer to be inside their sandcastles, which then serve to mark out their territory – define their particular space. Often these structures are so tightly packed together there is no room left to walk between them. In extreme cases non-Germans may find themselves sitting on bare rock, the Germans having excavated every grain of available sand for their Fortress Beach Towel.

Dream Inspired

The Germans enjoy escaping into fantasies whenever reality becomes too unpleasant. Failures and defeats require a metaphysical back-up system; they love to dream. The German equivalent of John Bull and Uncle Sam is sleepy-headed Michel, a name derived from Germany's patron saint, St. Michael. The poet Heinrich Heine summed up this propensity:

> The Frenchmen and Russians possess the land,
> The British possess the sea,
> But we have over the airy realm of dreams
> Command indisputably.

On occasion, the German fondness for escapism – their need for a spiritual essence – can make them seem other-worldly and impractical. Goethe noted wistfully, 'While we Germans torment ourselves with solving philosophical questions, the English with their practical intelligence laugh at us and conquer the world.'

The Ideal

'Nobody is perfect, but we are working on it', said Baron von Richthofen optimistically. Perfectionism is a prime German characteristic which benefits their auto industry, but can be a trial at parties. Compromise and settling for what is good enough is not good enough. Strictly speaking, only the epitome, the best, the ideal will do.

Furthermore, there is no doubt in the German mind that the ideal, or rather, the Ideal, exists and is out there somewhere in the ether. Naturally, here on earth, we can never achieve the Ideal, only a pale imitation of it. Plato may have been a Greek, but he thought like a German.

So it is not surprising that many Germans relate to ideas more than to people. As Goethe put it, 'The Experience is always a parody of the Idea'. Ideas are beautiful and don't let you down; people are unpredictable and do. Clashes between ideas and reality are inevitable, and Germans are quite resigned to this. It is part of what makes life tragic.

This is reflected in German literature and legend. Many German heroes fail because they measure their ideals against the imperfection of their nature and that of the world. Lamenting this sad state of affairs is a German preoccupation. Making the best of a bad lot and taking the rough with the smooth are more or less alien concepts to the German mind.

Beliefs and Values

The Germans prize *Bildung*, meaning education and culture. Showing off what you've read and what you know is not boasting. It is a way of participating in the nation's cultural life and taking pride in it.

Modesty in regard to education will not be interpreted by them as hiding your light under a bushel, but as an admission of ignorance. If you've got it, flaunt it.

Germans have unequalled enthusiasm for their cultural heritage. For many English people, culture is what the advantaged do in their spare time, and the idea of reading Shakespeare or Samuel Johnson for fun is rather remote. For the average German this isn't so.

Not to have read the whole of Kant's *Critique of Pure Reason* would surprise them (how could you allow yourself to miss out?), and they will have read Goethe and Schiller and Shakespeare with passionate, if uncritical, interest.

Religion

The Lutheran Church has had the greatest influence in shaping German attitudes. Luther's translation of the Bible shaped the modern German language, and it was part of his teaching that one's spiritual duties included obedience to worldly authority. In keeping with the Protestant work ethic, there is no very deep conflict between material wellbeing and one's prospects in the afterlife.

In Germany Protestants are in a slight majority (since reunification, which brought many East German Protestants into the fold). Broadly, the north is Protestant while the south is Catholic. The Catholic area coincidentally corresponds with the area under Roman occupation 2000 years ago.

Relations between the Churches are very good, with the spirit of ecumenicalism smiling benignly on all manifestations of religious life.

Churches are extremely well funded, the vast majority of the Germans gladly paying their church tax even if most of them seldom turn up at services. This accounts for the presence of so many Mercedes in clerical garages, but also funds enormous amounts of welfare work.

At home, church money supports hospitals, kindergartens, old people's homes and schools. Abroad, money is channelled into famine relief and Third World aid. The Germans have the best record in Europe on this score. Their preference is for steady, organized generosity rather than compassion binges of the Band Aid sort.

Class

Germany does not have a class system any more. The old distinctive class differences have been levelled out since World War II. Nowadays nearly everybody belongs to the same class, which by English stratification could be roughly described as upper-lower-middle-middle class.

A small but significant number of German aristocrats does exist, but like their English counterparts they keep very much to themselves, hiding their wealth, land and influence with an un-German-like lack of show, many even sending their children to English boarding schools.

Not every 'von' denotes aristocracy; that of the so-called 'vegetable nobles' only means 'from', as in 'from the village of'.

German aristocratic titles correspond to the British ones in name only. Unlike the British tradition of leaving the title just to the eldest son, aristocrats in Germany pass on the parental title to all children. As Germany used to consist of about 300 independent states, each with its own upper class, noble names have always been plentiful. Intermarriages with commoners can spread the name across all class barriers, especially since after a divorce the commoner is entitled not only to keep the title, but to pass it on to future spouses and children as well, who will also... etc. This accounts for the astonishing abundance of titles in Germany today. It is all part of a crafty scheme devised by the State to bring about such an inflation of nobility (at least in name) that eventually titles will become so common, they will be meaningless.

Wealth and Success

On the whole, the Germans are not ostentatious in displaying their wealth. On the other hand, massive gold jewellery makes a nice display and is ever so reassuring to have around. They appreciate quality, and are happy to pay for it. They are well dressed, well shod, drive solid cars, live in double-glazed and centrally-heated homes equipped with lots of reliable gadgetry.

In Germany money tends to act as a social leveller. Living standards are higher than in Britain, and the consensus is that anyone who has earned it and can afford it deserves the best. There is little of the snobbery that insists people should 'know their place'. If your prosperity is the result of your labours or wit, few will dispute your right to enjoy it.

Being Green

The Germans worry about the environment. Green economics and green politics are much more developed than in Britain, where the Green Party has only slightly more credibility than the Monster Raving Loony Party.

This particular preoccupation is founded on real concern. Industrial pollution is a major problem, much of it coming downstream in the Rhine, a river so full of chemicals that someone once managed to develop a photograph in water taken from it.

The state of many of western Germany's rivers is something of an own goal. Before reunification they exported most of their toxic wastes to East Germany, where a great deal was dumped unceremoniously into the nearest river, only to flow back into West Germany.

But what made the Germans really sit up and take notice was *Waldsterben*, the dying of the forests. The discovery that the economic miracle was killing their beloved forests gave the Germans a jolt they have yet to recover from. Forests, even if seldom visited, exert a powerful influence on the Germans. They are regarded as the natural habitat which most shaped the German soul. It was from the forests that they emerged to rampage across Europe and lay waste to Rome 2000 years ago and it is to the forest that they return (in spirit at least) when modern life overwhelms them with its horrors and demands.

Even today, around 30% of the land is covered with woodlands, and entering them gives the Germans a thrill of danger missing from their ordered urban life. The German forests are primordial and awesome. Their crisis is a crisis for the German spirit.

The Germans are keen recyclers. There is no shortage of opportunity to sift their green bottles from their brown, their plastic from paper. At supermarkets, people can discard the packaging and leave it behind altogether. Manufacturers of white goods (fridges, ovens) nowadays make efforts to see that the parts and materials they use can be recovered and recycled.

Green concern and the commercialism that surrounds it leads to some absurd situations. The scrupulously separated waste is quite often thrown together again when it reaches the dump, and none of it is recycled. And the demand for recycled paper is so great that the mills have to pulp perfectly good new paper to make it.

The Germans don't mind these imperfections in the system. Recycling is a beautiful idea, and that's what really counts.

Behaviour

The Family

The Germans are family orientated, though not conspicuously more so than their neighbours. The family is the ideal, the focus for *Treue* (loyalty), but divorce rates are high, as couples succumb to the ubiquitous stresses of modern life.

German society as a whole is not well disposed towards children. In public your dog will usually get a warmer welcome than your offspring. Children are regarded as noisy and disruptive, liable to interfere with other people's right to quiet and *Ordnung*. Some of this may be explained by the fact that as more Germans live in flats than houses, noise and disturbance can be more problematic. Yet in the home, family life is warm, affectionate and *gemütlich* (cosy).

For the Germans, the concept of cosiness is much more than comfort. It is interwoven with the idea of *Heimat* – the cosy heart and hearth of home and family, the safeguard against *Angst* and homesickness, the warm and orderly shelter in a cold and chaotic world.

Eccentrics

The Germans do not share the English taste for public displays of eccentricity. This need surprise no-one in a country where neighbours have been known to complain about the irregular way others peg their washing out on the line (and have even rearranged it in a more pleasing symmetry).

Fitting in is a virtue, standing out an offence. As a foreigner, should you don a Union Jack waistcoat and kiss-me-quick hat, pedal around on a tricycle bedecked in pennants, and carry a selection of your favourite mice in your pocket, the Germans will assume that you are bonkers but will smile indulgently. Similar behaviour in another German will have them tutting furiously, looking up the number of the asylum, and worrying about the effect on property values.

The Elderly

The Germans also differ from the British on the matter of the elderly. This is an old person's society. Germans only really come into their own after retirement, at which point they discover within themselves reserves of conservatism and a passion for *Ordnung* they had never dreamed of in their crazy youth.

To the average German senior citizen (and that is the only kind there is), life is a perpetual round of vigilantly seeking out infractions of rules and regulations, and helpfully (and loudly) pointing them out to the miscreants concerned. In Germany, the autumn of life is the most *ernsthaft* time of all, and you will never see a senior citizen smile or laugh in a public place (though they may permit themselves a wry chuckle in the privacy of their homes).

Other Germans treat the elderly with the deference and respect due them and eagerly anticipate taking their place among this élite.

Animals

The Germans are fond of their pets, which come in two forms – Alsatians, and preposterously small poodles wearing little woolly jackets and ribbons in their hair. The point of these creatures is to be Obedient and Loyal (Alsatians) or to eat expensive chocolates and pooh everywhere (poohdles). Saying anything rude (or even mildly critical) to a German about his dog is more than your life is worth. All dogs are beautiful, and the world is their litter tray.

Those Germans who do not own a dog are strange (and could even be eccentric). Those who own a cat are certainly Communists and may be cut dead in the street. If the man next door acquires a budgerigar or hamster, any self-respecting German will think about moving house (and perhaps going to another town altogether).

Immigrants

Unlike America or, to a lesser extent, Britain, Germany is not a melting pot where peoples from diverse cultures are thrown together to make the best and worst of it. Remarkably few people immigrate, in the true meaning of the word, to make their permanent home in Germany and to take up citizenship. Foreign workers in Germany all intend to go 'home' eventually, even if they stay for decades. They live in a sort of mental and cultural limbo, not wanting to carve out a place for themselves in German society, and not really expected to. Their rootlessness is caught in the German word which describes them – *Gastarbeiter*, guest-worker.

German treatment of minorities will always be scrutinised by the outside world. Encouragingly, the majority of young Germans are passionate about supporting minority rights and wanting a multi-cultural society.

The guests were invited, they do the jobs that Germans don't want, they have brought a degree of internationalism to a parochial society and have worked wonders for German health, bringing urgently needed relief from the national diet of unremitting stodge.

Gastarbeiter include the Spanish, Italians and Greeks – recognised as fellow Europeans, but also as Mediterraneans (good from a food point of view, but worryingly laid back on the *Ordnung* front). The largest group is the three million Turkish people, some now in their second and third generations in Germany. These groups have created a whole new social stratum, with distinctive youth cultures and their own German dialect, 'Kanakisch'. Isolated in German society for a long time, the *Gastarbeiter* are now more a part of the scene, with Kanakisch expressing characteristic lifestyles and attitudes, which are surfacing on mainstream television and in magazines.

The *Gastarbeiter* are less of a problem than the many people who would like to join their ranks. Countless numbers from the poorer and more oppressed parts of the world clamour to be allowed to live and work in Germany. The Ossie guards who used to be employed to keep people in, have had to be reassigned to patrol the borders to keep people out.

Why do the Germans envy the Chinese? Because they still have their Wall.

Manners

German manners are somewhat on the robust side. Don't expect an apology if somebody knocks into you on the pavement; what you'll get is a withering look for having had the selfishness and inconsideration to get in the way.

The withering look, a German speciality which you can observe children practising even in *Kindergarten*, is frequently accompanied by a muttered remark questioning the state of your mental well-being. It is a German quirk that these remarks are always couched in the formal '*Sie*', never in the informal '*du*'.

Even when he or she has elbowed you out of the way, trodden on your feet, glared at you and is calling you a moron without the sense of a dead dachshund, a German will always address you as '*Sie*'. It would be unforgivably rude to do otherwise.

Right to Wrong

You may on occasion be pulled up short by German bluntness and directness. The Germans are constitutionally unable to admit to being in the wrong or having made a mistake.

With their unshakable conviction that there is a right answer to everything, they have difficulty with shades of opinion. They will unhesitatingly express their disagreement in terms of your being wrong. Not, "I don't think you're right about that", but "That is false!"

If they don't like something, expect to be told so in no uncertain terms. Sparing other people's feelings is quite unnecessary since feelings are a private matter and have no business in public. While the British will engage in a form of agile verbal sparring, the Germans expect you to state your wishes clearly and directly, to use language at its face value. The Germans say what they mean and mean what they say:

"Do you know what time it is?"

"Yes, I do."

Queuing

The Germans are not great ones for queuing. At bus stops they won't entertain the idea on principle. It doesn't make the bus go any faster, and it doesn't help you get a seat, since that is down to the efficient use of elbows and withering looks.

In supermarkets they will queue, but grudgingly and only because there isn't any choice. In other shops, it is a matter of fine judgement. Queue-jumping might cause unpleasantness if the person you're planning to displace is in a hurry, or pushing a pram, or over 60, but otherwise it's open season.

This rather chaotic approach seems out of keeping with the demands of *Ordnung*. And so it is. It appears that because shops and bus stops occupy an ambiguous position in the public/private divide, they are felt to present opportunities for free expression of the self. But in the works canteen the queue will have military precision.

Greetings

The Germans will shake hands at the drop of a hat. Hand-shaking is an unavoidable fact of life, and you will do well to reconcile yourself to pumping the flesh on all occasions. You must shake hands on meeting, on parting, on arriving, on leaving, on agreeing something, and on agreeing to disagree.

The Germans believe in the firm handshake which, done properly, should dislocate at least half a dozen of the smaller bones. It is considered a sign of friendliness to hold the hand for an extended period. If someone is crushing your hand in a vice-like grip and won't let go even as stars dance before your eyes and you feel your life-blood ebb, this simply means that they like you.

While the handshaking element of greeting people has been perfected to a fine if excruciating art, Germans are rather less adept at introductions. If you bump into an acquaintance who has a stranger in tow, don't be surprised if you are not introduced. Your friend may well stop and enquire after your health and happiness, may even get deep into conversation with you. His companion will be left standing there inspecting his fingernails, polishing his spectacles and generally working his way through his repertoire of displacement activities as best he can. Your chum will ignore him with aplomb and appear not to be the least affected by his predicament. Yet don't be deceived. Behind the granite facade, your acquaintance will be suffering agonies of embarrassment and humiliation because he cannot think of a graceful or elegant way of bringing the stranger into the conversation. The root of the trouble here is that the situation is accidental and unplanned – something no German likes or feels comfortable with.

There is a telephonic equivalent of this failing. If your host takes a call while you are with him, he will never let his caller know that he has company. You must be prepared to settle back and wait while the interminable series of grunts and monosyllables which make up German telephoning runs its course. And don't expect any word of apology or explanation when your host finally gets back to you. It will be quite beyond him. Do the decent thing and pretend that nothing happened: your host will be unendingly grateful to you.

Formal and Informal: *Sie*-ing and *Du*-ing

The formal rules of etiquette are simple. When meeting someone for the first time, address them as '*Sie*' and continue to do so until the informal '*du*' becomes absolutely unavoidable (for example, while sharing the post-coital cigarette and enquiring politely about earth-movements, etc.). A general guideline is that when you move on to first-name terms, '*du*' becomes appropriate.

Social context will offer guidance: in business, never deviate from the formal. The Germans will remain on '*Sie*' terms with colleagues even after decades of sharing an office, and a boss calling his secretary by her first name will be universally suspected of having an affair with her. At radical student functions, informality may be the rule.

German reluctance to move on to the informal level reflects how *ernsthaft* a matter friendship is. Some Germans accomplish the transition by stages. To begin with, you will of course be addressed as Herr or Frau X. Later, should you discover sporting or other interests in common, and perhaps a mutual acquaintance or two, you may be addressed by your full name: 'So, Frank/Francine

27

Jenkins, I am very pleased to see you once more...' Finally, after many months or years, you will move to first-name terms, and '*du*' will ensue.

A variation on this, which should not cause alarm, is if you are called exclusively by your surname, 'Ach Jenkins, my old *Freund*!' It is essentially the same thing.

A distinct difference between English and German social life is the absence of petty hypocrisy. It is not good form to pretend to like someone for the sake of making a sale or gaining an advantage.

The strict separation of the public from the private provides a guarantee that in private the Germans are open and sincere. They may lack polite cushioning phrases, seeing them as a waste of language, and keep their distance from strangers and acquaintances much longer than the English, but when you cross the Hellespont of the '*du*' it means that all reservations are gone and you have made a friend for life.

Obsessions

The Germans are obsessed with many things: it is a form of recreation among them. The state of their own health and that of society are favourite topics for dwelling on, at length. Both, they are convinced, are on the point of irreparable breakdown.

Simply look at the front covers of the news weekly *Der Spiegel* for an update on the latest versions of these twin obsessions. 'Is Impotence on the Increase?', 'What's Going Wrong With Germany?', 'Death of the German Novel?' are typical cover stories. Inside they will be dealt with in depth, with many an opinion by experts (no self-respecting German has confidence in anyone but an expert). After 10 to 15 pages of minute analysis these articles come to no very firm conclusion beyond the certainty that things will go downhill from here on.

You may come to feel that the Germans are constantly in a state of crisis, and you would be right. German life is a permanent emergency, teetering on the brink of the unthinkable. Crisis is its life's blood.

Cars

A further obsession is their cars. The Germans love their cars more than almost anything. While the Italians reserve this kind of adoration for their children, Germans prefer to keep their children indoors, so the cars can play safely in the streets.

German cars are pampered, primped and squeaky clean. Only a real brute with no feeling at all (or a foreigner) would drive around in an unwashed car. Such a person could be sure of disapproving glances and withering looks wherever he went.

Some Germans don't just derive status from their cars, they take their whole sense of identity from them. Cars are not a matter of life and death for Germans, they are much more important than that. An Opel person is looked down on by a BMW person, while Porsche people may be suspected of being flashy fly-by-nights. Naturally, the stately, solid, dignified Mercedes rules the roost, carrying its costly cargoes of Herr Doktors and Herr Professors and Herr Direktors the length and breadth of the Republic. Without doubt your car says more about you than cash ever could, and can act a bit like a sign of the zodiac, embodying character traits and distinctive features which mysteriously transmigrate to the person behind the wheel.

Even great historical events are symbolized and encapsulated in car lore. The collapse of Communism will be forever linked in the German mind with the Trabants (universally known as the Trabis), which came spewing through chinks in the Wall as fast as they opened up.

This sad little vehicle, like a blender on wheels, seems to embody everything that was wrong with the old GDR. The shapeless body perfectly represents the grey uniformity and undifferentiated social structures of the failed socialist state. No space, no status, and precious little *Technik* with which to get the ever-desirable *Vorsprung*.

The Germans are utterly perplexed by the fondness the British and other nations show for this clockwork menace. For them it belongs on history's scrap-heap, along with every other reminder of the so-called Democratic Republic.

Leisure and Pleasure

Leisure is a bit of a problem for most Germans because by definition it consists of no-one telling you what to do or letting you know if you are doing it properly. In order to cope, the Germans do what they are best at: they make work out of it. Watching a German relax is exhausting, and you may need a day off to get over it.

You will never see a group of Germans simply lounging around the park catching the rays of a summer's day. Leisure time is an Opportunity for Improvement, so on Monday mornings expect to hear detailed accounts of how the classes in Old Icelandic are going, or what went on at the Motormechanics for Mothers self-help workshop at the weekend.

Sport

Sport is the perfect excuse for working all day Saturday and Sunday. The Germans do not really see sport as a means of character-building. In a highly competitive society, sport is a popular way to improve and display one's general fitness and performance in an organized fashion.

Every third German citizen belongs to a sports club. Football, also the main spectator sport, is a traditional passion, while tennis became an overnight success and Boris and Steffi were seen as national heroes and adored for their effortful superiority.

Clubs

The Germans love clubs. It is said that whenever three Germans come together they will find some reason to form one.

If you see a group of Germans on a street corner, they are sure to be on a club outing of some sort. Clubs abound: there are well over 10,000 choral societies nationwide, and all other interests are represented in comparable numbers. Many clubs have deep historical roots, as with the rifle and hunting clubs. Some of these date from the Middle Ages, and are swathed in guild-like ritual and tradition.

Clubbiness reflects the German dislike of doing things by themselves. Part of this is that they love organizing things. Frequently, the fun of being in a club is more to organize an activity than actually to carry it out. Every German's heart beats a little quicker at the thought of club business: committees, sub-committees, draft proposals, preliminary budget plans.

They love the opportunities for establishing status and doing a bit of social climbing. What nicer than being elected Club Secretary, Treasurer, Vice-Chairman, Chairman. All this is done in a spirit of great seriousness, and with the utmost conscientiousness. And if once in a while you have to go on a country ramble or do rock climbing or whatever, well, it's a price worth paying.

Clubbiness begins early. Since few schools organize sports, most of the facilities and training are available only through clubs. The habit is acquired early and lasts through life. It is by no means unheard of for someone to be buried with the insignia of their bowling or angling club, rather as certain football fanatics will name their hapless children after the entire team.

A uniquely German kind of club is the student fraternity which thrived in the second half of the 19th century. These are fundamentally drinking and duelling clubs but, being made up of typical males, everything is surrounded with all sorts of elaborate puff and ritual, including mottoes and monograms, coloured ribbons and initiation rites, and the singing of drinking songs. When a club member's honour was slighted in any way, a duel would ensue. The object of these was not to kill or maim but to scar the face. The classic image of the German aristocrat with a monocle screwed into his heavily scarred face owes its existence to the preposterous goings on in the student fraternities. Duels with sharp-bladed sabres are still fought as a test of courage.

One of the chief functions of clubs is to exclude others and offer identity and coherence to a group of people who otherwise may have little in common. A club also serves to lend a measure of dignity to whatever the members get up to. A lone Morris dancer may encounter laughter and ridicule, a group of 20 will meet with more respect.

A characteristically clubby phrase has it that '*hier sind wir unter uns*' (here we are among ourselves), a signal that you may let your hair down and enjoy yourself.

Sex

The Germans are as fond of sex as everyone else and remarkably tolerant of other people's foibles and peculiarities. There is great openness about sex – in-depth discussions about its problematic nature are inevitable wherever you go and any sign of embarrassment will be taken as a symptom of psychological hang-ups.

Seduction techniques leave something to be desired, and many Germans seem to rely on the age-old method of boring the pants off you. Once under way, expect full-blooded and vocal expressions of pleasure and delight (or disappointment), and don't be taken aback by frank comparisons of technique, duration, etc.

The commercial face of sex is coarse, vulgar and occasionally very strange indeed. For details, see Hamburg's Reeperbahn. In general, licensed premises and persons receive routine health inspections, thus reducing the risk of contracting any unpleasant surprises (but only slightly).

However, if you like your sex to be a mysterious smouldering ecstasy, choose the French. To the Germans it is more like an invigorating work-out in the gym or, in extreme cases, minor surgery.

Sense of Humour

The Germans take their humour very seriously. It is not a joking matter.

Harsh, astringent and satirical is their style. The cabarets of pre-war Berlin are famous. Their bite was ferocious: the nearest modern equivalent is the British *Spitting Image,* but this is playful by comparison. Classic German satire put the boot in and twisted the knife.

Humour is used by the Germans to come to terms with life's reverses and hardships. Most of them know that the best laid plans will probably collapse into ruin. This is all quite natural for, if a German maps out his morning or a weekend trip away and it all goes wrong, he will meet the disappointment with fortitude, a wry joke and the quiet satisfaction that he knows how ~~this wicked old world works.~~

The Germans don't view Sod's Law as the occasional irritant in the way the British do. Rather, it is seen as an Iron Fact of Life to which all must yield. If more than three things go right consecutively in a German's day it will occasion incredulous stares, astonished disbelief and fearful speculations about uncanny forces at work in the world.

The Germans' humour does not translate very well. Most German jokes when translated into English are no funnier than the average till receipt. Learn a bit of German, and you'll soon come to realize that there is a rich seam of humour running through German life. But their humour is largely a matter of context. There is a time and a place for being funny and for laughing. *Ordnung* decrees that humour is not the oil that makes the days run smoothly. You do not tell jokes to your boss (although levity with other colleagues may be all right at times), nor do you lard your sales pitch or lecture with witticisms. Irony is not a strong German suit and may easily be misunderstood as sarcasm and mockery.

German humour tends to have a target. After all, you don't throw a custard pie into your own face. While they are happy to laugh at others, and especially the misfortunes of others (other Germans, that is), their faltering self-confidence doesn't allow for self-ridicule. They do not joke about foreigners; jokes about East Germans only began *after* reunification. The butt end of German humour centres on regional characteristics: the stiffness of the Prussians, the brash, easy-going nature of the Bavarians; the bovine East Friesians, the quickness of Berliners, the slyness of the Saxons.

The Bavarians see jokes as a convenient way of taking revenge on their old archenemies, the Prussians. The Swabians don't mind jokes about their thriftiness, but prefer to be economical with them. Hence:

A Prussian, a Bavarian and a Swabian are sitting together drinking beer. A fly falls into each one's mug. The Prussian pours away his beer with the fly and orders a new beer. The Bavarian picks the fly out of his mug with his fingers and continues drinking. The Swabian picks out the fly and then forces it to spit out the beer it has drunk.

To help you get a joke, Germans will gladly explain it to you. If they are of an academic bent – or from Stuttgart – the finer points of the explanation will be repeated so that you cannot fail to appreciate it. For some Germans, humour is like a great painting, it must be planned, prepared for and built up in layers over a long period of time. For others, it is like the battered body of the Six Million Dollar Man; they have the technology and they will rebuild it so that it is better than nature made it. Either way, a joke or a shaggy dog story will be polished and honed, refined, revised, improved, re-worked and bettered in every possible way – until it is absolutely perfect and quite incapable of raising a titter.

Part of the problem is that most Germans apply the rule that more equals better. If a passing quip makes you smile, then surely by making it longer the pleasure will be drawn out and increased. As a rule, if you are cornered by someone keen to give you a laugh, you must expect to miss lunch and most of that afternoon's appointments. If you're lucky you may get home in time for *Nachbarn* (*Neighbours*).

Humour in Germany is also subject to an official timetable. A good example is the custom of the *Karneval* celebration which is particularly popular in the Rhineland. It starts officially at 11 minutes past 11 o'clock on November 11th (no insult to Remembrance Day is intended, it just happens that 11.11 is a very orderly numerical combination to the Germans, and order is also pivotal to emotional enjoyment).

Pageants, parties and performances continue for some months, all with the official obligation to be funny. To avoid disorder, strict rules have been set up to organize the merriment as efficiently as possible. During congregational speeches, which are endless concoctions of jokes, every joke is marked by an orchestral signal so that nobody will laugh at the wrong moment. Disorderly humour is not only nothing to laugh about, it is often not even recognized.

Culture

German culture is for the most part earnest, and big. Not for them the slender volume of elegant stories beloved of the French. Nor do they like the wry observations of village life or frail metaphysical puzzlings of the contemporary English novel. Germans want value from their *Kultur* and *Kunst* (culture and art), and value means bulk. No would-be cultural icon can get away with a small oeuvre. Just look at what they're up against: Collected Works of Goethe, 143 volumes – even workaday selections will weigh in at anywhere between 15-50 volumes; Collected Works of Nietzsche, 30 volumes at least; Wagner's operas, two weeks' listening if you don't break for meals or sleep; *Heimat I, II* and *III*, as long and convoluted as life itself.

It is perhaps because paintings can't be long that the Germans have never really gone in for this form of expression. But buildings are quite big, and you may expect excellent architecture, old and contemporary.

The trick when confronted by all this massiveness is not to be intimidated. Break off a manageable chunk. Suck it and see. You will be pleasantly surprised – at times, astonished.

German culture in general and literature in particular is different from others in two main ways: it is comparatively young, having only really got going during the 18th century, and it is highly self-conscious, with characters in plays even from the 19th century stepping out of the framework of the drama to complain to the author or argue points with members of the audience. It arose in response to a powerful sense of inferiority that there was no body of specifically German art, and a creeping *Angst* that other nations might regard the Germans as philistine.

The man who changed all this, and who dominates German culture like a colossus, is Goethe. Almost single-handedly he gave Germany a literature to be proud of, comparable with anything the French, the English or the Italians can offer. He put the Germans up there with the best of them, where they have ever longed to be. He seemed to contain the entire German *Seele* (soul) within him, and for this he is cherished, loved, adored.

Ponderous German scholarship has almost hidden him from view. This is a shame, because there never was a livelier, more fascinating writer. He brims and fizzes and bursts with energy and ideas. His intellect soars with the exuberance of a champagne cork in flight. He contributed new and extraordinary things in poetry, novels, drama, travel writing, autobiography. With something to say about everything, his ideas range from the dazzling to the downright daft.

In his youth, Goethe was a star without parallel, the Michael Jackson of his day. When he dressed a character in his first novel in blue and yellow and had him commit suicide for unrequited love, Europe's youth donned blue and yellow and penned tragic farewells. In old age he was the grandest of old men, and all his conversations were taken down verbatim. Hardly a day of his life is unaccounted for, hour by hour (i.e., 'Goethe: The Missing Twenty Minutes').

Goethe is the German Shakespeare, and Shakespeare,

too, is a sort of honorary German thanks to the classic translation of his works by A.W. Schlegel and L. Tieck. '*Sein oder nicht sein*' (To be or not to be) echoes around many a packed house, and lots of Germans think of Shakespeare as a German who simply lived in the wrong place.

On the whole, it is not recommended that you come to German literature looking for a happy ending. You won't find one. Happy endings are not *seelenhaft*, or soulful, and certainly not serious. German art is introspective, brooding, self-obsessed: in a word, German. The message is more important than the medium; heavily indigestible (but brilliant) ideas. The core is what matters, not the outward shell.

The Germans love philosophy every bit as much as they love literature. *Dichter und Denker* runs the phrase, meaning Poets and Thinkers, cultural heroes both. The philosophers to crib quotes from include Fichte, Hegel, Kant, Leibniz, Nietzsche, and Schopenhauer – heavyweights besides which French or English philosophers can only be awarded a contemptuous sneer.

The 1950s and '60s saw an outpouring of plays and novels chronicling the *Angst* Germans felt in relation to their unresolved past and in the face of the material success, but spiritual emptiness, of contemporary society. Political themes also came to the fore, with some of the best writing coming from East Germany.

The Germans need a small, restricted, clearly defined area of chaos to offset their sense of order. The cinema offers it. After the work of directors like Fritz Lang and Leni Riefenstahl, the emergence of a new and radical cinema rather startled everyone. Fassbinder, Herzog, Schlöndorf, Margarethe von Trotta, Wim Wenders and others have produced a series of extraordinary, bleak, bizarre and intense films which deal with German themes, or wider ones, in a uniquely German way. They might be tough to sit through, but they pass the test of being *ernsthaft* with flying colours.

Intelligence is an Intelligence Test

For the Germans, what you read equals how smart you are. Turn up on the train with the latest Jeffrey Archer and you'll find out pretty quickly what being ridiculed feels like. Germans don't read for pleasure; they read in order to be intelligent – or at least seem to be so. That's why German novels are sold by the kilo. Pick up the German edition of something familiar and reassuring by, say, Raymond Chandler, and you'll be in for a shock. It will be printed in minuscule type densely packed on the page and conveying the visual impression that this is an academic treatise.

German readers are happiest when they know that every penny spent on a book has bought them an hour's worth of hard, self-improving labour. Nobody seeing you read impenetrable jungles of verbiage could possibly doubt that you must be very brainy indeed. Well-spaced lines and big friendly margins are banished as offensive indicators of being lightweight.

You can get around this ghastly fact of life to some extent by reading foreign literature in translation. Flaunt something extremely slender yet profoundly marginal – in English or French or, better still Russian or Japanese – and German admiration will know no bounds. They will assume that if you're reading thin books it must be because you've already polished off all the fat ones, and if you're reading foreign books you must have exhausted all the German ones.

Television

German television is lamentable. The staple diet consists of dire imports from the US and the rest of Europe, dubbed with ham-fisted insensitivity. It can come as quite a shock to see your favourite serial in Germany, the characters growling and squeaking in a variety of unlikely tones.

German continuity announcers are inhumanly silken-voiced and slick. You will be continually addressed as 'Ladies and Gentlemen' and 'Honoured Viewers', and the evening will pass with a series of chiming noises and strange pauses during which nothing happens.

News programmes and documentaries are long, painstakingly thorough, and wearyingly stuffed with politically balanced expert analysis.

Programming for children is among the best in Europe, so adult taste for old-fashioned items is a surprise. There are times when you simply cannot escape the welter of black and white minstrels, barber shop singers, and pseudo glamorous circus-style big band shows.

German television has always been responsive to the needs and wishes of the young. Even in the early 1970s, German youth had access to far superior popular music shows, where they could see and hear not just banal chart favourites, but cult 'underground' acts like the Grateful Dead, Velvet Underground and the other exotic oddities of the era. Perhaps this is because any manifestation of culture, no matter how awful, might turn out to be 'important', in which case to have ignored it would be mortifying. Better cover it, just in case.

Conversation and Gestures

'Small talk' is an expression which has no direct equivalent in German. People would be mortified at the suggestion that any utterance they make is less than portentous.

The English compulsion for discussing the weather is looked on with wry compassion. Germans prefer their informal exchanges of opinion to concentrate on more worthwhile and serious matters – like the enormous strain they are under, the terrible pressure of work, their appalling hardships, the manifold symptoms of their stressed condition, doomsday and other uplifting topics.

Other popular themes are holidays and how much you need one, how much you had to work last week, why you really need a holiday now, why you have to work even harder this week and how to interpret holidays and work in terms of Planck's quantum theory, Hegel's idea of the absolute or the new tax reform – topics which should be approached with the utmost circumspection lest you are suspected of being sarcastic or trivial.

The polite English 'How are you?' is likely to be answered with a comprehensive, head-to-toe survey, taking in all the bodily systems and missing none of the major organs. If you don't want to know, you'd do well not to ask.

Insults

The Germans dearly love to swear and curse, and have any number of explosive epithets with which to do it.

Bodily functions are graphically referred to whenever anything goes wrong. *Scheisse* (shit) is used so frequently and by so many people that many Germans are not even aware that it is a swear word.

If you call a lady a *Dose* (literally a can), she will slap your face, while no gentleman will tolerate having his *Schwanz* (literally tail) referred to in public.

The legal consequences of verbally insulting another person can be severe. Should mutilation or disablement result from an accident or crime the victim receives small financial compensation, but hefty fines result from publicly questioning somebody's intelligence, such as pointing at your forehead – the derogatory gesture popular with motorists that suggests someone has taken leave of their senses. The Germans take care not to indulge in trading insults in the presence of the police.

The middle finger raised is equivalent to the English 'V'

sign. Three fingers extended to form a 'W' used by neo-Nazis is strictly prohibited (as is any Nazi symbol, the salute or the swastika – even on a toy model of a Messerschmitt). The gesture most frequently displayed is the raised index finger. In every German there lurks a lecturer, longing to get out.

Custom and Tradition

The Germans value customs and follow them assiduously. They love traditions and have plenty of them though the majority are of local rather than national origin. Most are a more or less elaborate ritual preparation for the consumption of enormous amounts of beer.

Many customs and traditions are linked with the ubiquitous clubs. Rifle clubs, *Trachtenvereine* (clubs for the wearing of local traditional costumes), pigeon fanciers clubs, all have their festivals which may typically consist of beer drinking, a religious ceremony, beer drinking, a parade, beer drinking, and be rounded off nicely with a glass or two of beer.

For the ceremony of *Richtfest* (roof-topping), which marks the completion of the roof timbers before the slates are laid down, a party is given by the house-owners for their friends and neighbours, and the builders. Much beer is consumed. Finally, a beribboned wreath or small tree is fixed to the summit of the roof, to let everyone know that the work is going well and that the owners have done the right thing.

Harvest time and the business of wine-making and brewing bring festivals to celebrate nature's bounty. The greatest of these, the Munich Beer Festival, *Oktoberfest*, is famous the world over. Over 16 days, locals and visitors down enough pints to keep a small country going all year, and make a serious dent in the chicken population. To keep them in the mood, there is much jovial arm-linking and singing of boomps-a-daisy German songs while swaying to and fro hoping not to fall over just yet. If you have ever longed to dress up in *lederhosen* and tunic or dirndl and frilly bodice, and bob about in a tide of large bosoms and bellies, the *Oktoberfest* is for you.

The majority of customs and traditions are linked to the Christian calendar. Notable are the celebrations before Lent. These have their origin in ancient fertility ceremonies for welcoming the returning spring, and retain their pagan character. They usually feature some variation on the carnival Prince, Princess and Peasant (always men, even the Princess) who are the presiding spirits of *Tollität*, or madness.

Ascension Day (*Himmelfahrt*) was traditionally cele-brated by the men going off together on elaborate outings to the countryside, to picnic, tell tall stories and imbibe a few. The women stayed at home, enjoyed the unwonted peace and quiet and doubtless celebrated with a drop or two themselves.

During the *Tolle Tage,* 'Crazy Days', of *Karneval*, *Ordnung* goes out of the window and the entire ethos of German workaday life is turned upside down. But on Ash Wednesday, everyone is back at work in a very *ernsthaft* mood indeed, ready to knuckle under for another year.

Christmas

Christmas is the main focus for tradition and custom, and is every German's favourite time of year. The British Christmas is a pale and thin imitation, which owes what little *Gemütlichkeit* it has to the efforts of Prince Albert to bring a little cheer to the benighted country he was married into.

Advent is marked by decorating the front door with a

wreath. Indoors the children are given an Advent calendar, so they can enjoy the count-down by opening a little door each day to see some Christmassy picture or find a little sweet. On the mantelpiece or dining table, another wreath is placed which has four candles on it for lighting on the Sundays; first one, then two and so on until all four are lit the Sunday before the big day.

In the run-up to Christmas, most towns have a Christmas market in the town square or outside its main church. Here you can find all manner of cheap and cheerful trinkets for sale as well as spiced cakes, punch and seasonal sweet treats, plus a funfair and Christmas carols played by musicians in the church spire or some other conspicuous place.

St Nikolaus Day is celebrated on December 6, a sort of dry-run for Christmas. Children are required to put a shoe outside their bedroom door the night before, which is then filled with goodies while they sleep – provided their behaviour during the year has merited it.

The distribution of presents is a rather formal event on Christmas Eve. Children are banished from the house (or at least kept out of the living room) in the afternoon while the tree is set up and decorated. Tradition requires a dinner of carp, but this is generally held to be so unpalatable that most people opt for roast turkey, goose, venison or sausages instead.

Eating and Drinking

German food has a poor reputation, being held to consist of fat and carbohydrates and very little else. It has been said that to the French the quality of food matters, to the Germans the quantity, while the English are concerned with nothing but table manners.

The Germans do not scoff constantly, but once their eating gains momentum it's hard to stop. Overdoing it is a German habit, and not only where food is concerned.

Part of the German reputation for greed stems from the fact that before, during and immediately after the Second World War food was scarce and poverty was rife, so that meals were monotonous and small. As food returned to the shops and cash to the wallets, the Germans embarked on an orgy-gorgy of epic proportions. This became known as the *Fresswelle,* a tidal wave of face-filling over-indulgence which produced the quadruple chinned generation which constitutes the very stereotype of the German physique.

Eventually the Germans came to terms with the coronary consequences of their less than delicate eating habits. Where once they ate about three times as many potatoes as the British, they now eat twice as much health-giving fruit and fibre-rich veg. Today, the label 'light' is a sure-fire sales booster as the younger Germans determine to avoid ending up like their barrel-shaped elders. There are even 'light' mineral waters boasting less carbon dioxide.

One preference remains unchanged. Germans eat more pork than any other European country, 4½ million tons of it a year, or the equivalent of 5½ ounces of pork per person per day. The Germans have an old saying: 'One cannot live from bread alone, there must be sausage and ham as well.'

The German breakfast will feature orange juice, fresh coffee (not instant, *danke schön*), a choice of bread with a selection of jams for the sweet-toothed and hams, salamis and cheeses for those requiring something a touch more substantial. German bread comes in all shapes and sizes, and in a good many colours, too. In fact, about 200 different kinds of bread are available, and the Germans are very partial to wholemeal (no health fad, this, they have always liked it that way). From rye bread to Pumpernickel, *Schwarzbrot* (black bread) to pretzels,

German bread is a meal in itself.

Mid morning, the Germans like to snack so that they don't expire before lunch which is the most substantial cooked meal of the day. Mid afternoon requires you to stop what you're doing (unless you're at work) and go in search of *Kaffee und Kuchen* – 'coffee and cake'. The cakes will be enormously elaborate affairs layered with fruit, cream, chocolate, cream, sponge and perhaps a little more fruit. Extra cream is served as a matter of course.

Supper* is called *Abendbrot*, indicating that bread and cold cuts are again the order of the day, although cooked meals are common, too. Then before bedtime you may like to eat a little something just to keep night starvation at bay. Of all the worries you may have about Germany, the fear of going hungry has the least foundation.

Drinking

One in three of the world's breweries are in Germany. This alone should tell you what the Germans think about beer. Not so much a way of life, more the be-all and end-all of it.

Small, local breweries manage to survive and thrive not just in ones and twos but in droves. Beer has a traditional association with monasteries, where much of it used to be brewed. It has been classed as a basic food, and even prescribed as medicinal (as stout still may be for the British – though prescription charges make this an expensive way of enjoying a Guinness).

One reason German beer is of such high quality is the

---

* You may be surprised at the early hour (from 6.00-7.30 p.m.) at which Germans eat. No dinner at eight for them, let alone the Mediterranean habit of sleeping all afternoon and eating at midnight. Germans want to get it over with: they've got work to do.

German Beer Purity Regulation, laid down in 1516 and unaltered since, which states that only water, hops, malt and yeast may go into beer. The only time the majority of Germans expressed serious doubts about being in the European Community was when the Eurocrats tried to tell them that this law had to go in the interests of regulatory 'harmonisation'. The Eurocrats soon backed down. So, while some 4,000 brands of pure German beer are offered, all imports have to be specially labelled to warn of their impure and contaminated state.

Beer is always served cold with a generous layer of foam. Such an orderly head can require up to eight minutes to be poured and is not recommended for thirsty drinkers in a hurry. The most popular beer is 'Pils', which is also the number one export in contrast to 'Export' beer which is hardly ever sent outside the country, and 'Alt' (old) beer which is drunk as young as possible.

German wines are excellent and, unlike the Californians who more often choose French over their own, are deeply appreciated by the Germans (although the French turn up their noses at them). Wine drinkers and beer drinkers are identical in Germany, there is no either–or.

Despite, or because of, being such a boozy lot, there is no toleration of drunkenness on the roads. Limits are lower than elsewhere, and penalties stiffer. Eat, drink and be merry – but take a taxi home.

Health and Hygiene

Virtually all Germans have health problems, and if they don't, there must be something wrong with them. Most of what ails them is stress related. No nation was ever more stressed (*strapaziert*), but this is understandable. After all, running Europe can take it out of you.

The delicacy of the German constitution has long been recognized, and smoothly running systems have long been in place to bolster it and keep it going. In the 1880s Bismarck set up a national health insurance scheme because he worried that the workers might get *strapaziert* by the demands of flourishing industrialisation. Today the national health insurance underpins a vast and wonderful network of doctors and hospitals, specialists and spas.

Like the French, the Germans devote enormous resources to the treatment of an illness which doesn't exist, in this case the notorious *Kreislaufstörung*, meaning disruption of the circulation. While the rest of us go to meet our maker when our circulation stops, the Germans routinely recover from it and go on to lead useful and productive lives. Once they are good at it, the Germans can have a *Kreislaufstörung* as often as twice a month without it seriously impairing their social life.

Treatment for this frightening disease varies. It has been shown to respond positively to three weeks on a Greek beach, and the prognosis isn't too bad if you take plenty of pills and potions. (It doesn't really matter what pills and potions, the secret lies in ostentatiously stopping work and lining up an awesome array of small brown bottles on your desk before swallowing six of everything and sighing copiously.) Only one instance of someone actually dying because of *Kreislaufstörung* is recorded, a sad case of a young man whose pill-taking regime was so complicated that the schedule simply left no time for taking meals.

If *Kreislaufstörung* is an ailment which properly belongs in the realm of ideas, the main health worry for the Germans in the real world is the condition of their hearts. For the generation who took part in the *Fresswelle* this was with very good reason. The veins and arteries of these lumbering, wobbling colossi were choked and begging for mercy. Thrombosis was an ever-present threat. However, for their jogging-suited, water-sipping successors, concern for the heart is less warranted and has taken on a hundred shades of metaphysical *Angst*.

Because all Germans pay around 13-14% of their income into health insurance, German doctors are very pleased with life, and drive some of the newest and shiniest Mercedes on the roads. Dentists are so highly paid their main problem consists of finding sufficient deductible ways of spending to offset against their taxes.

In addition to six weeks' paid holiday, the Germans are entitled to a staggering six weeks' paid sick leave per year; and if you can fool them into it, the medical insurance companies will stump up for a further 78 weeks over a 3-year period. All this costs a fortune – social security spending swallows about a third of Germany's gigantic GNP, and cutbacks are taking place, cautiously. Everybody in the government knows that it is safer to steal a lioness's cub than to come between a German and his medication.

Spas

A uniquely German institution is the spa cure. It is conclusive proof of earnestness and *Seelenhaftigkeit* (soulfulness) to recognize the need to repair body and mind, and shoot off to one of these spas at the State's expense at the first sign of a sniffle or an ingrowing toenail. Once there you will wallow in special curative muds and drink unspeakably foul waters, in between taking moderate exercise (i.e., walking to the cake shop and back) and playing the time-honoured game of How Much Schnaps Can I Sneak Before Herr Doktor Notices.

A curiosity of the regulations governing being sent on a *Kur* (cure) is that you are expressly forbidden to take your husband or wife, on the grounds, presumably, that you need rest and recuperation, not to be nagged or to have to submit to Unreasonable Demands. In Baden Baden, where the wealthy take their cure, the mixed sauna acts rather like a butcher's display, allowing you to inspect your bit of rump steak thoroughly before buying. The consequence is known as the 'Spa Romance', from which patients and divorce lawyers both derive much solace.

Older lavatories in Germany have a curious ledge in the bowl. This puzzles and distresses many foreigners. What is it there for? The answer is the extraordinary curiosity of the Germans concerning everything to do with their health, and the fact that, should you spot some abnormality, it could provide the key to any number of weeks off work and a bit of slap and tickle at the *Kur*. Simple, really.

Hygiene

To the Germans, hygiene is the basic requirement of life and the absolute starting point of *Ordnung*. An unwashed German is a contradiction in terms, like a faithful Frenchman or a good English café.

In a German bathroom cabinet you will find a dazzling array of preparations and pieces of precision engineering for maintaining the human form in pristine condition. Dental hygiene takes pride of place. Only the very poorest of Germans will have one toothbrush, the remainder boast whole banks of them, with mirrors on sticks and high-speed water jets for persecuting every last molecule of plaque.

The tendency in modern homes is for each member of the family to have their own bathroom because the morning routine is so drawn out that sharing has become impossible; the last in line would simply never get out of the house.

Germans are passionately fond of every form of tonic and pep-me-up. They will swallow every conceivable kind of plant extract and animal gland, and will never doubt the good it is doing them, provided only that they have paid enough for it and that it tastes vile. It's all they ask.

What is Sold Where

On the whole, you will find German shops formal and a bit stuffy. The cheaper kinds of department stores are an exception. They resemble a poorly organized jumble sale, and jumble sale rules apply, so wear shoulder pads and a protective helmet. Elsewhere the standard of decorum is such that you are expected to keep your end up by dressing smartly just to gain entrance.

The German-style chemist shop is the apothecary, a mysterious place where there is virtually nothing on display beyond perhaps some dentifrice or manicure equipment. Behind the spotless counter is the spotless white-coated apothecary, as *ernsthaft* an individual as you'll meet anywhere, to whom you tell your woes and who, after some pretty close questioning, produces the sought-after box or bottle. Many of these shops are venerable and old, wood panelled and lined with marvellous glass or ceramic jars. They are a trifle intimidating with their sombre medicinal atmosphere, but if you're feeling frail, a visit to the *Apotheke* will be balm to the soul.

Opening hours for shops are strictly regulated. An exception is made for those supplying travellers with what they need en route. Making the most of this legal loophole, petrol stations have vastly extended their once limited stock (road maps and oil) and have sprouted mini-supermarkets stocking everything from biscuits to barbecue briquettes. Among their most popular items are beer at night and fresh rolls on Sunday mornings.

To cash in on the act, one enterprising German baker transformed his cake shop into a 'petrol station' by installing a battery charger for electric cars. The only electric car in town happened to belong to his father, but the baker got his licence and on the trading day he gained is happily making extra dough. In Germany they don't let the grass grow under their feet.

Systems

The Germans appreciate a system. There's nothing quite like having a system, if you ask a German. Systems make the world go round.

Take their motorway system. Germany's autobahns came into existence because Hitler wanted to avoid his tanks and armoured vehicles getting stuck in traffic. He also had an unemployment problem to solve. It seemed a good idea at the time, and proved its worth as a peacetime amenity. Getting around was easy and quick. Since then, getting around has become harder but that is due to the volume of traffic, not the roads.

The original autobahn system was an elegant one; in the former East Germany parts of it can still be seen in near-pristine condition, cobbled slip roads and all. Naturally, the Germans are working furiously to upgrade these old relics and prepare them for the road haulage avalanche which the development of a market economy has necessitated.

German law decrees that on the autobahn no speed limit applies, although there is a politely 'recommended' limit of 80 miles per hour to which only first-time visitors pay any attention. To the Germans this unexpected freedom from restraint represents an important niche of liberty in an otherwise red-taped society. The freedom of the open road, the opportunity for self-expression by slamming down the accelerator and leaving the rest standing, is cherished. You can see the gleam in their eyes, and stuck fast in the sweltering tail-backs which characterise so many German roads around the big cities, you will have plenty of time to do so.

The Germans have some unique regulations governing filter lights. The only way of coping is never to place yourself at the head of any queue of traffic; then you can just do what other drivers do, safe in the knowledge that none of them is likely to bend, let alone break, any of the myriad codes of the road. (By law, cars must even be furnished with a pair of surgical gloves.)

If, as a visitor, by some misfortune you find yourself first in line at the lights, your best bet is to abandon your car there and then; it will be infinitely better than facing up to the barrage of hoots and roars of those behind you.

Public Transport

The alternative is to go by bus or tram or train – every one of them a model system of efficiency and cleanliness.

The trains are fast and punctual, partly because stations are sensibly placed in the centre of towns and cities. The intercity services are known as IC, and the new intercity express service ICE is very fast, and features luxuries like fax machines, telephones and video.

In many of the cities confusion awaits you at the tube station. Do you take the 'U' Bahn or the 'S' Bahn? The 'U' Bahn goes underground while the 'S' Bahn goes overground. Except of course when it's the other way around. For maximum convenience, the 'S' Bahn seems to stop at most of the places where the 'U' Bahn does (though not the other way around, the 'S' Bahn reaching the parts other Bahns can't).

On certain stretches your 'S' Bahn ticket will cover you for travelling on the 'U' Bahn. On other stretches, it won't. Similarly, you may be covered for some bus routes and may even be able to take advantage of the excellent though dwindling tram service. But then again you may not.

Don't look for signs to explain it to you, there aren't any. Don't bother asking the ticket salesman even if there is one, the explanation will only baffle you more. Play it safe and buy whichever ticket includes everything – the extra expense is well worth it. Otherwise, walk.

Education

The German education system is not concerned with character-building or instilling moral fibre. Instead the aim is to load you with qualifications which will earn you respect and promotion in the market place.

Education for the Germans starts late and finishes even later. Nursery school is optional, primary school starts at the age of six, and the average student finishes university in his or her late twenties.

At ten years old the brighter pupils go to a *Gymnasium* (which is not for training the body but for training the mind) leading to university. The rest (some 60%) go to other secondary schools which are likely to take them towards an apprenticeship – a highly formalised three years in a shop, bank or whatever, including weekly theoretical training in a State-run vocational school. For many this leads directly into a career. Achieving the German *Abitur* (the final examination) automatically guarantees a place at university in almost any subject you like. If your average isn't good enough you may have to wait a few years, but rejection is not on the cards.

The Germans have to do National Service, being drafted as soon after their 18th birthday as school allows. You may object to military service and be given civilian service instead; but if you suffer from flat feet or bad sight, you are let off both. Some are lucky enough to avoid either, if the year's intake is full.

Qualifications

Every German you encounter professionally will be thoroughly trained and qualified. Degrees are coveted. An academic degree is prestigious and must be prominently displayed. Still more desirable is a doctorate. Being entitled to style yourself '*Doktor*' lends power to your elbow in every sphere, be it business, finance, the law, even medicine. It is not thought in the least odd to call somebody 'Dr. Dr.' if they have two doctorates, and good manners require you to.

Top of the tree and most prized is the professorship. If you come up against someone called Herr Professor you know you are dealing with a true heavyweight. Professorships are usually hard to come by, requiring a lengthy, complicated thesis and giving weekly lectures (sometimes without pay) while waiting for a professorship which may never turn up. Academic titles can of course be acquired with less effort by buying them, and this is regularly done by ambitious people in a hurry. Pretty much any title is available for a price if you know where to go (most commonly a third world country), and this form of aggrandisement is not illegal.

Money Matters

Most Europeans find it hard to feel sorry for Germans who are depressed over the current economic gloom. After all, what constitutes hard times in post-war Germany would strike many as a boom-time bonanza. Nevertheless, many, if not most, Germans will lament how suffering under the yoke of the economic convergence criteria is the Beginning of the End or the End of Everything (according to whether you are talking to an optimist or a pessimist). They are quite unable to see belt-tightening today as an investment for prosperity tomorrow. As always, they are cursed with being able to penetrate deeper into the meaning of events than anyone else, and so are wreathed in Wagnerian apprehensions of the *Götterdämmerung* kind.

To the Germans money represents security. Fear of losing their beloved Mark prompted them to question the value of European unification. Obviously sacrifices would have to be made, but preferably not on the financial front. Twice in the 20th century, after the First and the Second World Wars, Germany was hit by devaluation. Inflation reached astronomical proportions in the early 1920s. The majority lost all their savings. Even today, inflation is seen as the ultimate economic chaos, something to be restricted at all costs. The shock of it still lingers in the German soul.

Banks therefore play an even bigger part in business life than elsewhere. A system of 'universal' banking means that the banks own everything the government has not already got its hands on. In Frankfurt, the European Central Bank rules supreme, following in the footsteps of the Bundesbank. The Deutschmark may be dead but the Euro is looked to for a glorious German future, dominating everything in sight and running (not ruining, as some have maintained) the entire European economy.

Government

Germany is not only the Land of *Angst*, it is also the Land of the *Land*. Before reunification, there were 10 *Länder* (11 if you include Berlin). The NBLs (New Federal Lands) make it 15 (16).

Each *Land* is a politically separate region, with powers and responsibilities laid down by the Constitution, and each is represented in Berlin, in a rather ambassadorial manner, competing with the others to secure its interest at Federal level.

Federal Government is in charge of things like foreign policy, defence, taxes and telecommunications, while the *Länder* call the shots in the matter of education, policing, broadcasting and local government. Federal and *Land* governments go halves in splitting tax revenues, although by law no *Land* is allowed to become significantly richer (or poorer) than another. If they do, they have to hand it over.

The *Bundestag* is the highest law-making body. It elects the Chancellor (equivalent to the Prime Minister) who is the leader of the party with the largest number of seats, and safeguards democracy by allowing minority groups the right to demand information and ask for committees of enquiry into any funny business.

The *Bundesrat*, the upper house, is made up entirely of *Land* representatives, so the *Länder* can make their presence felt by influencing Federal legislation in the *Bundestag*, the lower house. For some legislation, agreement of the *Bundesrat* is necessary, for some not. Where it is not, the upper house can object to proposed laws, and even take matters to a conference committee where both Houses are represented and a compromise can be hammered out.

German Law is *Land*-based, with the exception of five supreme courts and the federal constitutional court, which exists to ensure that all legislation is compatible with the Basic Law which was set up at the same time as the Republic itself.

The President of the Republic is an elected figurehead, who may serve for a maximum of two five-year terms.

The system of *Länder* and central *Bund* is held in high regard throughout Germany, and *Land* politics are lively and of interest to most ordinary citizens. Many of the country's brightest and wiliest politicians are to be found at *Land* level, and have no very pressing desire to get into the Federal scene.

Officialdom

Bureaucrat heaven. Remorseless regulations, rigid rules, punitive, petty, pernicious, pernickety. A nation held together with red tape. Did you ever doubt it?

Crime and Punishment

It will come as no surprise that the Germans are keen on law and order. 'There must be Order' is the phrase on many a German's lips. To ensure that what must be is, the Germans are willing to sanction some fairly heavy-handed policing and some very strict laws.

Adhering to rules can appear to rule out reason. In the early hours of the morning at a deserted intersection, a man crossed the empty street without waiting for the green signal. Halfway across he was knocked down by a car speeding round the corner, which made no attempt to avoid him. The police were called, the man put into an ambulance, and the driver of the car was sent on his way without so much as a caution. Shocked, the only witness (a foreigner) wanted to know, "Isn't the driver going to be prosecuted?" The policeman replied: "No. But, if he survives, the injured man will pay a fine of 25 Euros."

Policing is the responsibility of the various regional authorities. If you decide to make a break for it after brutally dropping your sweet wrapper in the street, and succeed in getting as far as the regional border, your case will be formally handed over to the police in the next *Land*, who will take up the chase.

The Germans must always have their identity papers with them to avoid being arrested and locked up for up to six hours while someone goes to fetch them. If they move house, even one house further along the street, they must register their new address within a few days. No citizen can escape the long arm of the law for long.

German law can seem like a nightmare of pettiness and vindictiveness. One individual was fined because in remonstrating with a policemen he had used the word '*Mensch*', equivalent to an American saying 'Man'. No-one may imply that a policeman is a human being. Policemen are carefully vetted and if they show the tiniest sign of a sense of humour, they're out.

Law and order apply in the home too. Laws concerning noise and disturbance are rigid and, by others' standards, intrusive. Generally, all noise must cease after 10 p.m. If you live in flats, don't sing in the bath late at night, in fact, think twice about having a bath at all, and as for flushing the lavatory... Care is needed in the sensitive matter of when you cut your lawn since doing it at week-ends will probably get you into trouble, but not doing it at all will get you into worse. The safest bet, as indicated earlier, is to assume that everything is forbidden and against the law unless you have documentary proof to the contrary (in contrast to France where everything is allowed, even if it is forbidden, and Russia where everything is forbidden, even if it is allowed).

One of the more depressing aspects of German life is that all Germans love to point out to you what you are doing wrong or what you are failing to do right. Thinking of sneaking through a red light? Don't do it. A hundred Germans will helpfully call out that This Is Not Allowed. Thinking of leaving the kids' toys out on the front lawn? Don't do it. The whole neighbourhood is itching to point out to you that This Is Not Allowed.

German rules and regulations have proliferated so much and involve such unlimited red tape that the Germans have introduced a de-bureaucratisation law to cope with them.

Business

The majority of German companies are small to medium sized, old, and family owned. The relationship between boss and employees is close and friendly. The owner usually knows precisely what goes on at shop-floor level, having worked there himself at some time.

Industrial relations have always been much better and more stable than in Britain. Bosses and unions don't necessarily admire each other, but the need for co-operation and partnership is universally recognized. In German companies everybody from the chairman to the tea lady is called a *Mitarbeiter* or co-worker, and this is not mere rhetoric. Manual workers are probably earning comparable wages to management and enjoying the same conditions and benefits (not as a privilege but as a right). More importantly, both will regard themselves as social equals.

In business, seriousness and qualifications rule the day. Amateurs won't get a look in, and specialists can get no job outside their area of expertise. If you're a Doctor of Philosophy and can't get a post in a university department, you will probably end up working in a semi-skilled position. Business won't touch you with a barge pole.

The Working Day

At the office, punctuality is next to Godliness, although only the bosses are expected to be in early or to stay late. Most Germans knock off at 5 o'clock sharp. Working late is seen as an admission of inefficiency (which is Not Allowed), unless you choose the option to come late and leave later, or come early and leave earlier, which is known as 'gliding time'.

Plenty of loud grunting and complaining lets everyone know that you are exerting yourself to the utmost in the cause of *Gründlichkeit* (thoroughness). Quiet efficiency will be unnoticed by your superiors and earn you withering looks from your colleagues.

Ambition and competitiveness are the expected norm and their outward signs are intensity of effort and not sloping off every 20 minutes for a cigarette and a read of the newspaper. Performance, skill, achievement and workmanship are all highly valued. If you generate a mountain of paper and memos, you are clearly working hard and good at your job.

In the old days, Germans seemed to live entirely for their work. Since finding out about foreign holidays and 101 things you can do in a tracksuit, they have become less dogged. This has led to much national anxiety and articles in *Der Spiegel* asking, 'Are We Germans Becoming Lazy?'

Occasional after-hours jollies have to be put up with, but mixing socially with your workmates is fairly uncommon. Office 'do's' are pretty formal events. You are not expected to get legless and grope the canteen staff.

German business meetings stick to the agenda so as not to waste time; they therefore need extensive agendas. Time is precious, time is money. It is not to be wasted frivolously – until someone finds the perfect opportunity to 'profile' himself and begins to hold forth on everything he knows.

Women at Work

German men have always known that German women are a force to be reckoned with. Today, business is feeling the benefit as well, as women move beyond '*Küche, Kinder, Kirche*' (kitchen, children, church).

Women make up 40% of the workforce. Germany now has more than twice as many female Members of Parliament as Britain, and equal opportunities and treatment for men and women are demanded in the Constitution. However, men still occupy most senior positions. Only about 4% of all top posts in industry and commerce are held by women.

Language and Ideas

In their hearts the Germans believe that no foreigner can speak German properly. (In fact, they believe that only people from their own region speak decent German. There is nothing more barbarous to a Berliner than the Bavarian version of the language. Bavarians heartily reciprocate this feeling.)

German is a remarkably flexible language, and one in which new words are easy to make up – you simply take two, three, or pretty well any number of existing ones, and stick them alltogetherabitlikethis. This doesn't just make a nice new word, it introduces a whole new concept, perhaps explaining why the German psyche is so fearfully complicated. For instance, in a park the notice *Astbruchgefahr* registers in one swift glance that you are within the orbit of 'branch-dropping-off-danger'.

An alternative to this is to take a string of words, chop out all the bits you don't care for, and glue the remainder together. This is a popular way of coping with the names of government departments and so forth – hence *Stasi* from *Staatssicherheitsdienst* (the State Security Service of the GDR).

The German printed page is startling at first. The words are so long. A newspaper article may consist of just four or five words, yet take up two columns. The same is true of sentences and paragraphs. Look at a book by Thomas Mann. A thousand pages divided into half a dozen paragraphs.

Unsurprisingly, the inventive German tongue has given rise to many ideas and notions contained in one word, which are unmatched in other languages. For example:

Realpolitik – The pursuit of political advantage or survival in a tough world. Saying, "No, really, it doesn't hurt" after your hippo-like boss has trodden on your foot.

Schadenfreude – A joy-in-destruction sort of emotion which perfectly captures the surge of satisfaction you feel on hearing of another's downfall. Other languages are very coy about honouring such a caddish feeling with a whole word of its own. Consequently, everybody uses the German one.

Weltschmerz – It's a freezing February night, the central heating has packed up, your team is facing relegation, you've just been handed your redundancy notice and arrive home to find that the dog has been sick on the sofa. What you feel is *Weltschmerz*.

Frömmelei – The saccharine-coated piety typified by tele-evangelists who tell you that God urgently wants you to send them money, and who are subsequently found in bed with three people called Tammy (only two of whom are female). In relation to culture, it describes people who have never read Shakespeare, but refer to him reverently as 'the Bard'.

Kleinkariert – This literally means having a pattern of small checks. Its proper use is for describing the sort of person who has gnomes outside their bungalow and has holidayed in Frinton for the last 25 years.

Zeitgeist – Nothing less than the Spirit of the Age, and the cue for no end of sighing and looking world-weary. An invaluable word to use whenever German cinema or the music of Stockhausen are under discussion.

Vergangenheitsbewältigung – The sum total of difficulties a nation encounters in struggling to come to terms with a dodgy past. Who but the Germans would have a word for it?

The Authors

Benjamin Nicholaus Oliver Xaver Barkow is a German of the old school. Born in Berlin in 1956, he spent his formative years lobbying to have a wall built through the city because he strongly disapproved of the way the Socialists pegged out their laundry.

With this achieved, he moved to Hamburg, but finding it such a well-ordered place, moved swiftly to London. What he found there has so appalled and fascinated him, he is unlikely ever to leave. After a tempestuous and *Angst*-ridden adolescence, he studied humanities (in the vain hope that some of it would rub off). For most of his adult life he has freelanced as a researcher and writer, and has recently completed a history of the London Wiener Library.

Despite being a chronic sufferer of *Kreislaufstörung*, which no herbal remedy has yet cured, he soldiers on in the hope that one day he will understand why people don't understand him; at which point he will take his *Seele* out of pawn, move to the mountains and begin work on his cherished project, *Wagner, the Musical*.

Stefan Zeidenitz is descended from an old German family of Anglophiles who sadly failed to catch the last Saxon long-boat to Britain by some fifteen hundred years.

He has compensated for missing the boat by immersing himself in Far Eastern studies and promoting Japanese culture in England, English culture in Germany and German culture in Japan. In consequence, his sense of direction is sometimes slightly distorted.

The effortless superiority he encountered while teaching at St. Paul's School and Eton College has not yet super-seded his Teutonic temperament. But he is working on it.